AMBASSADOR OF NUMB

AMBASSADOR OF NUMB

SUSAN SCUTTI

SHANTI ARTS PUBLISHING
BRUNSWICK, MAINE

AMBASSADOR OF NUMB

Published by Shanti Arts Publishing

Designed by Shanti Arts Designs

Cover image— sebastian-schuster / K18B4Y4LAbl / unsplash.com

Shanti Arts LLC
193 Hillside Road
Brunswick, Maine 04011

shantiarts.com

Printed in the United States of America

ISBN: 978-1-962082-91-4 (softcover)

LCCN: 2026930708

To my ancestors

CONTENTS

ACKNOWLEDGMENTS

The author extends her gratitude to the editors of the following publications in which these poems first appeared:

2 Bridges Review: "Slum"

ANYDSWPE Anthology 2014: "And So the Train to Brooklyn" and "Subtraction"

The Christian Science Monitor: "Direction"

The City Key: "During the reign   of restlessness" and "Hudson Chapel"

Eratio: "Like Childhood or an Army" and "naivete"

Far Out Further Out Out of Sight: "Relations"

The Genre Society: "Ambassador of Numb"; "Flawed"; and "oocyte"

Loose Change Magazine: "Told to a Stranger Far from Where I Live" and "Told to a Stranger Far from Where We Live"

Night of a Thousand Poets Anthology: "Recovered"

Oxford Review: "Living Among Indians in Journal Square"

Tamarind: "Film Noir"

Tin House: "Unmanned"

Tribes Magazine: "And After This What?"

White Rabbit: "Seed Bomb"

PART ONE

RELATIONS

In the living room the mother and the daughter sit side by side chatting like sisters. The mother arranges the umbilical noose like a strand of black pearls around the daughter's neck. The daughter laughs and moves the bowl of fruit—glistening berries which appear pregnant in their ripeness, just ready to burst—beyond the mother's reach. As time passes, the shadows in the room deepen, eventually darkness covers each face like a veil. In the cellar desperate impulses gather like mice. The mother tells the daughter to close the curtains and turn on a light. Completing her task, the daughter climbs the stairs and returns to her attic, tucking her wings beneath her on the bed. The mother sighs then dons her mask, traveling deep into another mind to disappear.

ATLANTA QUINTET

with a passing ice cream truck
the mechanical notes of Maple Leaf Rag
blow open the stained curtains

wings of a jasmine-scented breeze

❋

sun melts beyond the farthest houses
small figures alight on skeletal branches reaching across the sky
a dissonant soundtrack begins

how raucous evening can be
in the place where birds flock for winter

❋

I don't avoid the boys
smoking in the park after dark
my insipid smile ensnares them with neighborly regard

I am the mugger
come to rob their ability
to inspire fear

❋

a rising moon dangles
before the child's outstretched hand

an abrupt wail
as unfulfilled desire
is tasted for the first time

✿

during a humid night of erratic sleep
a beetle crawls across my kitchen counter

lying in bed
I feel the insect's
movements
in my bowels

FLAWED

The daughter   is busy though her two hands are idle, useless as suspicion.
On the horizon   the father crests a wave and swims to shore. He walks
toward her, blue   veins visible in the high arches of his feet. The
daughter's eyelids   flutter like a sleeper descending into REM as the father
steps between bodies   littering the beach. The ocean thunders against the
shore. He'd left a bread   crumb trail but the path home had been
consumed by hungry birds.   Mostly the father felt discontent. A sheen of
sweat veils her brow as the   daughter travels deeper into memory. Pain in his
eyes: poverty pain, war pain,   pain mass-produced and spilled onto the
conveyor belt of his genera-   tion. "A little more water," he told the daughter
as she stirred cement in the   red wheelbarrow.

She learned a fistful of scien-   tific words to explain an ending where his mind
eroded while his body remained   intact. Soon plaque and tangles suffocated
the neurons that controlled his   breathing. He turned blue when he died, a
stillborn baby. For too long such   recollections corrupted her vision of the
father. Today she must use her   earliest memories like clay, like bricks, to
recreate the man he once was.   Build a house of him. Here is his door, she
says thinking of his tears. Here   is a window made from spit. Carefully,
ceaselessly, she rips his image   from her womb, becoming mother and daughter
both. I sing the body electric.   (She unravels cables to wire him.) I sing the mind
electronic. Now she falters.   The spell broken, her eyelids flutter, her hands
blunder and then halt. In a   flash she sees the ceiling must be cracked. Must!
His final illness is essential   and without it, the house will be incomplete. The
crack conjures eternity, it's   the defect that reveals divinity.

AND SO THE TRAIN TO BROOKLYN

muzzled urges animate a shuffling crowd
celluloid vendettas unspool within Bluetooth silos
a stranger, bowed by private grief, passes
unremarked

PREMONITION

The region of your mind where instinct lives
has been buried in moss and
transported to an occupied city.

Your heart speaks now in
participles you understood as
a child, your hand trembles

as you receive
the photograph of
billowing clouds beyond the school yard.

Within the frame of this future afternoon
you will be comforted by
strong arms.

It's so easy to love
with no prison in view
and even when hail begins to fall

all that is
between you
remains uncomplicated.

Isn't it true that we have all been here before?
As a child, you never dreamed of
violence or murder but now your

mind is filled with
thoughts of war
and on what day will you depart?

Why are you here—a
face misplaced amidst the
simple doom of poppies?

FILM NOIR

Expensive sins flicker within the depths of her eyes as
she joins the busy-minded crowd commuting through
daylight and Styrofoam take-out.
He reads her like a prescription, notes
potential side-effects before
dosage and refills. His desk chair squeaks, a hairline fracture
divides
the window.
A passing piercing siren completes
several pirouettes in the dusty office before
fading into the distance. Her skin is as pale as unfed
dreams, her eyes wet
with unvarnished need. The false
notes of her coloratura work as counterpoint to
his bass decency. Plump enough to conceal
a Glock,
her purse rests in her lap like a pampered Pekinese.
A manicured hand flutters to her mouth,
covers an asthmatic cough. Turning to go,
her profile is as pretty as a lie told within an adulterer's bed.
Amber fluid laps against a bottle's inner shore
as he opens his desk drawer.
The splash in his throat is cheap enough to be memorable.
He pockets her check bearing a Rorschach signature
foretelling violence
and
unspoken regret.

SUBTRACTION

A part of you is unborn
a slender fold tucked within your mother's womb
where you remain hidden from ambition and anger.

Meanwhile the rest of you lives
a blameless existence in a city
where distortion is a general tendency.

Daily you listen to the sounds of
individual resolve and collective aspiration
going flat or sharp unexpectedly.

Tonight a man accepts your dollar bills —
unclean and crumpled like
used tissues.

He stares with dark eyes
that speak a familiar guttural
language of neglect.

Returning to your pillbox apartment
you turn the deadbolt,
silence the phone.

Folding yourself into cold sheets,
You float into
the amniotic silence of sleep.

AMBASSADOR OF NUMB

nightfall   you sit in a room peopled by fictions while outside
thunder sounds like splitting wood   your daydreams resemble
faces in the windows of a passing bus   it is the forgotten
anniversary of an unremembered encounter with a complex
personality   and afterward what remained was lifted and placed
on a high shelf   for years you have succeeded in evading
recollection   yet without your knowledge or permission it has woven
itself into the fabric of your temperament   and so you are
compelled to begin an argument of hatchery: Is connection necessary?
Why him?   meanwhile your family. Your family and their
values like unavoidable purchases of shampoo and soap   the
email you receive from your sister ends with a phrase: "I will pray for
you."   her prayers pursue you like official documents, her
prayers intercede on your behalf, you are a stamp in her passport of good
intentions   with nothing more to do your brain imagines her
brain   the idea of you that was born in her left hemisphere
travels the corpus callosum to the right   and there it resides, waiting to
be redeemed within this foreign lobe   so you sink into a fissure
creep among the crevices   and soon disguise yourself as shadow among
synapse

FISSURE

How casually we meet
to put aside sorrow

and take up intoxication which
unravels our thoughts

until nothing is left but
a desire to grasp

what is not known.
Together we will move

deeper into what cannot last
while the beat of an abandoned heart

becomes the gentle tempo
of our dance.

FIFTH MONTH IN SIBERIA

The blanket worn over his coat
smells of cabbage soup.
"...simple penance of memory," writes Razumihin,
lifting bloodshot eyes to the
fractured window. In the hazy light,
his hand has an appearance of
wax. Meanwhile, his brother-in-law
remains a malnourished
thought.

Hatless, Dounia rushes
through damp
alleys, unflattering
streets. Dead leaves chatter against cobblestones.
Pressed against her right lung is
a blood-stained purse filled with
unspent coins. She purchases sighs and
weeping in her nighttime dreams...
a Saint Petersburg
wedding cake iced with
grief.

"...desperation leading to an
exacting justice..."
Razumihin's pen, mouselike, continues to scratch.
In the street opposite his window, a shrieker
runs her fingers through tangled
hair, straightens her apron, prepares to
beg.

Dounia rattles the brass
handle of self-examination before entering.
Uninvited thoughts collapse onto the frayed upholstery
of her mind as, wide-eyed, she
paces the dusty carpet.
Razumihin busies himself by
shelving groceries.
When his wife finally tires, he cautiously defiles her qualms
before restoring her wavering, wandering
faith.

OOCYTE

How long
till the blunt faces
on the train evaporate from memory
only to melt into the unremembered stations of
your daily commute? Not yet nightfall, you linger on a
park bench.   This late afternoon is ripe for delight:
sleeping swans float on a pond's smooth surface, a yelping
poodle parades at water's edge, barely visible stars puncture a
crayon-colored sky.   To think it all began for you with
physical contortion.   Two bodies askew on a bed, internal
logic forced, liquid perimeter trespassed and multiplication
commenced.   Separation undone, a new
singularity is created.   How is it that
the geometry of beginning is somehow
always equal to the compulsion
to end?

SHE WHO IS MADE TO FURNISH EGG AND CHILD

On her fingers is the scent of onions.
In her mind stirs a faceless god.

Beneath her heel an insect writhes.
On her lips is a ready lie.

Within her dreams she has not yet fallen.
In her hair a colorful, chemical dye.

This complicity with nature is essential nature.
Capacious ambition, remorseless vision,

Her choice
To choose or strive.

AFTER READING ABOUT RIOTS IN LONDON STREETS

On 10th Ave
where this city's infrastructure unfurls
like a concrete mobius strip daydream,
where accordion-waist buses jostle bumper-to-bumper,
an asthmatic horse passes.

Dappled gray and dragging
anachronism,
the beast ripples in clipclop heat,
a madness identical to your own
glistening in its shuttered eye.

(This not-pretty day is already
half-mast and
yet to be seized.)

As you pause to stare at
this Apocalypse minus three,
an animal scent lingers
on the wind.
For weeks now you've watched as
cruelties accumulate on TV.
Hopeless inactivity has been planted
everywhere yet you consider yourself lucky to encounter
riot-less-ness.

Such strife
will transpire, at least for now,
in another city in another country
that is an island not unlike your own:
mother tongue, paternal temperament.

Still, you aspire to a gleaming future.
though you feel homeless
within snug domesticity,
colonized once again by a chaos as
inevitable as a Canal Street
knockoff.

Victory may be bitter-sweet but still it can be had here.
Here, where acknowledgement is too often mute
and savage.

HUDSON CHAPEL

Maneuvering like
atomic particles, seafarers
ready their
kayaks as a
bird pirouetting on
the branch above my
head begins its
strange call: a drilling
sound as persistent as
examined conscience. Forlorn
industrial structures
squat on
a pier to my left while
a lone
seagull, impervious as
false confidence, floats toward
me along the tide.
It is assumed small
birds possess
no malice, no charity, no philosophy ...
but how do we know?
Someday scientists
will view the
unconscious mind with special
instruments just as today they
inspect someone's internal
organ— a liver, say, or
a heart—with contemporary
machines. The kayakers
in dayglo life vests grow smaller
as they glide into the distance.

Overhead
the motor of an airplane
drones and a fly, its
transparent wings twitching, lands within
the shadow
of my foot.

A woman and her
husband in early old age are
speaking in Russian as
they approach. The
woman passes
three empty
benches, then sits right beside
me . . . crowding me.
She turns and
says "Gud mohrnink" with a smile. In a
gentle voice her
husband scolds
her for her
sweet moxie which, glancing at
me, he understands I
forgive-respect-admire. On
the breeze, I smell
her, her
scent is not unpleasant just
dissimilar to my own. I suspect
she eats more meat than I do. Pickled or
otherwise prepared parts, perhaps
livers or maybe
hearts, the discarded
organs of the same
animals I
consume on occasion.
Exhaling, I watch the narrow houses

perched on a cliff across the river.
They stand isolated yet together,
whispering confidential secrets into
strong winds. Meanwhile
peace, random
yet always certain, arrives to bathe
the island, a scene of
colluding energies, as we three
sit side by side
observing.
Melville,
how right you were
to send Ishmael
to the sea, the sea
the sea:
strange mirror
of self-
discovery, a
bewildering pulse of
eternity.

BOY

He wears headphones,
Someone else's rapped rage rotating through his mind.

Nightly, the Morse code of simulated gunfire falls on deaf ears.
His games are a
Imagination atrophied, he dreams in shades of blue, the same blue
as the light seeping through the crack beneath his bedroom door.

Junior year's one approachable teacher produces a photograph.
As evidence.
I am waving, explains the boy to a (purchased) counselor. Not saluting.

Athletic trophies rattle on glass shelves as he passes.
Piss puddles on classroom floors.
The rifle is nearly weightless and as slender as the ribs protecting his heart.

He bullet-sprays blackboards,
leaves illegible hieroglyphs,
mementos of his massacre.

LIVING AMONG INDIANS IN JOURNAL SQUARE

A car alarm went off and gave everyone a start
Three pedestrians bumped into one another, hostility aroused yet
Not one of them blamed the absentee owner of the impressive vehicle
Which shimmered in the lingering sunlight bookended by
One dull gray SUV and a scuffed white pickup
Two locavores unconsciously smiled as they loitered nearby
Beholding such elegance sitting within reach
In ways it looked exactly like every other thing that is unwanted and left
By the curb and I said so to the butcher who frowned as he
Stared through his shop window at all of those
Passing by

It is a mystery to me that machinery fascinates so many people when
You can buy a talking birthday card for a couple of
Bucks are so mysterious when you happen upon them in the woods
Antlers like family tree branches and startled awareness in their eyes
Masks for perfect instinct like the closed blinds behind which I sit as I
Remember you telling me about a subway stop in Rome where you
Descended how many flights? into a milling darkness
As dramatic as the sudden wail of an expensive auto abandoned by
Who knows
Who

I can no longer wait for someone to turn up and turn off the noise
If perfect peace does not exist when you arrive I will close all my windows
So you will remain undisturbed by sounds from the street
Let me apologize in advance for any obvious lack and please know that I
Appreciate your subway story and I thought of it once when another nearly
Perfect stranger said, "I do not believe in the human soul" as I stood
Waiting on the platform, poised between
Him and
Obscurity

WE ARE

up
close
the flowers
reveal
individual
dispositions
frayed edges
of a
tulip's
petals
downturned
face
of a sunflower
meanwhile
the feathered
discussion
continues within
the
strongest
branches
of the
rooted
tree
mysteries of
similarity
and
heartfelt
anomaly

EMMA STORY

In
the
museum
one woman
watches another
woman study a third
woman's portrait. The
standing woman's oblong
eyes narrow as she bends to
inspect the brush strokes in a cor-
ner of the canvas. Last month she left
her longtime boyfriend for a younger man
who doesn't know her well enough to remind
her of her failures. (Yet.) In a year her pregnant
belly will swell like a sail filled with wind. Now she
is unknowingly or possibly rudely blocking the other
woman's view of the portrait. No worries: The seated
woman is daydreaming about leaving the guy she's been
involved with, an unfailingly kind carpenter, to take up with a
lecturer in fractal geometry. She met the new guy on a plane to
Helsinki; during take-off, she spilled coffee all over his pants. Two
weeks from now, sharp abdominal pains after lunch will send her to
the ER where her appendix will burst while she is waiting to see a doctor.
After this *health scare* (more like *death panic*), her feelings for the carpenter
will deepen like a teenaged boy's voice. With this change of heart she'll return
to this very spot, unknown forces drawing her back to the portrait. The subject is
a woman who attended the New York School of Art and then married another painter.
The canvas shows this artist seated at a piano, her face suffused with love as she looks
at George Bellows. Seeing the picture again without someone blocking her view—without
the distraction of her romantic triangle—the woman wonders: Where are *Emma's* paintings?

LIKE CHILDHOOD (OR AN ARMY), THIS WINTER

will be replaced by
another face
worn beneath your mask
and all that you love will pass away
in time or
truce.

Regret is without use or
ceremony. Behind
unnoticed door, a man
discovers the antennae of
his thought.

Minds were manufactured to meld and
retreat, repeating each synapse of
conspire.

Do you know where your song begins?

It is here
where you fear
conclusion dwells, here in muddy
boots cemetery puddled and
here, too, is where the spiral recurs —
a revolution
as earth on
axis continues
its clandestine orbit, this continent
splattered across
its shiftless face.

HAPPY PEOPLE DON'T PLAN WARS

instead they sit in snug rooms
contemplating the flavors of impending meals
the pleasures of smoke and red wine
(flowing in a way that is not at all like
blood)
and once sated they
co-exist without rancor
and make love
or at least conversation

why are so many never schooled
to understand that
this, *this*
is exactly what life can be?

enjoyed so as to avoid
unnecessary pain

no child alone
with stick and stone

ESPERANZA

the woman has made repeated mistakes and run   now she rides a
 train to and from work   it glides back and forth across the
same tracks, a tongue sliding in and out of a mouth   each morning
and night the woman sits across from someone new as the train
continues   it is an elaborate tale told by a pathological liar   a
young girl sits across from the woman   she is murmuring   and the
noise of the train drowns   her words   at night on the way home, a
heavy set man has fallen asleep   his yarmulke is slightly askew and
in the artificial light as the train speeds through a tunnel the woman can
see a fastening clip   it gleams like a fallen coin   the woman once
wore a similar clip in her own tangled hair   she can no longer
picture her younger face   was she one of those kids that looks
hopeful?   these days she understands there is something bad inside
everyone   in the evening she passes a laundromat with a Spanish name
inside the people drift   like clouds   back and forth they move
between noisy, metal machines   it is their calling, their
preoccupation   washing sweat from garments made dirty with their
labors   they're mining for goodness

DURING THE REIGN   OF RESTLESSNESS

The only open seat
is beside a questionable
person. Wilting
you ease into the
space beside him.
He asks if you have
a habit.
"A habit
isn't a bad thing," he says. "Some people live their whole
lives with a habit."
The train you ride causes a strong wind as
it arrives in the next station.
On the platform, a woman's hair
rises and falls like an empire.
The phone you clutch carries a message
that you're unable to delete.
Other things you cannot discard are mistaken ideas about
the rich and casual slights by so-called friends.
Camera-ready smiles appear genuine
despite the vacancy of eyes tucked within
layers of makeup.
"We are troubled by behavior
that does not align with our own:
Your assignment for today is surrender."
A slender shriek escapes your lips
while you doze among the beginnings and endings
of things discovered within
the night's fragrant pulp.

UNMANNED

In the backseat the sister, who will one day become a sodden wife occupying the largest house in a college town, hits her younger brother. He reacts without thinking and punches her back: one solid thump on her gingham thigh. Indignation, stronger because it is unjustified, singes the sister's pale complexion. Although she is in her first year of high school, she whines to her mother who is anxiously watching the road. "Brake, brake!" the mother tells the father, a careful driver who has done nothing to provoke such anxiety. (The father presses the gas.) Pretending not to notice his parents, the brother stares at a passing brick building and silently vows never to marry. From the fourteenth floor, the roof of their car is the size of a fingertip, their intertwined antagonism a line of dirt beneath the nail. The woman observing the car steps back from the window and presses her own fingernails against her eyelids. Now she is a pink-eyed monster sprung full-grown from an acid trip. "We," she says into a phone, "dropped bombs and afterward the pilots left their remote-control station and returned home in time for dinner." She is talking about drones. She is talking about past conflicts. She is talking about residual damage and moral injury. She and her boyfriend split up half a year ago and yet she is still parroting him to her best girlfriend. Aware of doing so, the woman wonders about the nature of power. Immediately, her memories skip to her past: she is standing at the ocean's edge watching her father swim beyond white caps. Seeing the strength and determination of each of his strokes, she steps into icy waters and follows him into the breaking waves.

THE URBAN WOMB

In this oldest of neighborhoods
within an architecture of mislaid pleasures &
forgotten impulses
you found your voice.

(or *a* voice)

& this has made all the difference
in a life that continues to unspool like
a thread . . . a threat
of something fearful, something
future

& so you commence another genetically modified feast

Meanwhile.

Banks mint bigger banks,
their cash flows an artificial menstruation
bloodying the legs of each borough
as trucks reverberate along the avenues,
sirens filling the hollows.

Sap rises in a deformed tree.

(Aren't all cities identical? Fueled by
self-congratulatory fevers,
each success is similarly addressed.)

Who are you when no one sees?

A slender wafer on a receptive tongue
you dissolve...
all doubts subverted by the robed priest
chanting beside an altar where
no visible sacrifices
are made.

THE DAILY NEWS

There's so much dust in the air even though it's been days since the workers first arrived. They jackhammered, shoveled, hauled away rubble and then climbed into a hole they'd made in the tarmac. Each evening—after emerging from subterranean depths but just before leaving, streaming east along the avenue in their acid yellow vests—they arranged thick metal plates to cover the cavity. Yesterday, after a moon appeared between buildings and began a wayward journey across the sky, an occasional truck would hit those loose metal plates at just the right angle and make a shockingly loud noise that flew skyward and then landed in my apartment.

Today, as I hurry outside my door, the breeze is cool with a hint of wetness. I'm rushing, eager to walk along the river flowing just beyond the highway. Once there, I parade, prancingly, along the path where other people pass, pausing briefly to observe a man on a bench who appears so purposeful with his head bowed as if in prayer.

Meanwhile a tough and fearless woman walks a tough and fearless dog while birds provide sound-bytes from nearby leafy trees. What could they be saying? *Let's eat worms. How do you like my nest! Is each of us really free, free, free?*

Walking north, I approach an unexpected crowd clustered in the area between the ferry terminal and the *Intrepid*, rising like a dull gray whale from the green water. A woman stands on a platform shouting into a microphone, her words flapping in the breeze like laundry on a line. I see an opening, enter and begin to thread my way through the clustered listeners, but I get only so far before I am blocked by a phalanx of strollers. Turning back, I am careful to avoid stepping on scattered belongings or getting tangled in the large red, blue and yellow flags held aloft by raised arms.

Reaching the perimeter, I glance backwards and see an elderly man hopping on and off the curb like a cricket, his cardboard sign bobbing up and down with his movements: Long Live His Holiness the Dalai Lama.

Why do I remember, all at once, a forgotten moment?

Entering a building through revolving doors, I'd checked in with security, taken an elevator to a high floor, and then taken a seat among the unemployed waiting for an interview. Each person who passed wore a corporate

I.D.

hanging in its plastic lanyard from their necks. Cowbells is how they looked and those of us waiting stared dumbly at the sight. In this alternate universe—waiting to break out of our eggshells like so many hatching birds in this skyscraper nest—it was impossible to not feel united. Loosely speaking, we were Those Without an Official Identity. Our private thoughts pooled like water around our feet and each of us prepared a piecemeal personality arranged like a metal plate to cover whatever lies beneath.

The thought passes. I am once again walking north along the river. A diesel scent is on the wind as the distance between me and the past grows.

> the river
> scented and silent
> attentive to itself alone
> bathes this island
> of traffic and noise

A NEW MAN

His grief had formed itself into
Critical anger.
It had the heft and balance of a baseball bat.
He used it to bash at the world.
A war is coming in Europe, he told her
While she lay under the covers hiding from the cold
Unable to make anything of the hours
Between work and sleep.

Her father had been an angry man
Though playful, too, but only in rare moments
Usually the minutes spent outside the house
And well beyond the family.

You think you always have to be happy, her father once said to her.

Do you want riots across the nation? the other says to her now.
The new man, so unlike her father except for the grief:
Grief for battles lost, love that never came.
Grief for ashen dreams.

Grief wielded like a club.

SALT & SILICON

Icy waters surround an accumulation of concrete and separate experience.
Splayed against the sidewalk, your shadow refuses to leave you.

What lingers beneath the rippling surfaces of the sea
Lapping at your boundaries of discovery?

You remain confident even though electronic reach
Exceeds your imaginative grasp.

You occupy a room suspended high above the earth's surface.
Each Sunday widens and curves, minutes amassing in the dishpan.

Your middle years are tarnished with an accretion of shame and responsibility
while alienation follows occasional bouts of vulgarity.

Once again, you taste the unsatisfying draught of carbonated deity.
Once again, chill winds discover the island of your face.

COLLEGE REUNION

Looking down from high windows I witness
Sunset and shadows that
Unmoor the silent-seeming park
From all that is molten beneath

✿

The sudden and brief display of maxillary canines when asked about his
Profession

✿

An innuendo of interior life
Stains the end table
An implication of unsatisfied thirst
Ripples venetian blinds

✿

I am this and not this
You are this and not this
We are this and not this

✿

The one who serves
Smiles
Another who does not
Frowns

✿

Do you fear a wage-
d war?
Or is your worst worry the prospect of spiritual loss?

✹

A pantomime of familiarity
And kaleidoscope of confident chatter
Stalls the arrival of trust

✹

Sudden return of a long-forgotten memory
Brings us
Nearer
An unknowable sky

PARANOIA

The truck, which is unusually clean, possibly new, has small tanks affixed to its side and the back appears to be filled with sand. Looking into the street from the second-floor window of the gym, I can see only part of the driver's face. The tanks, glistening in the sunlight, contain unknown liquids and the tarp that partially covers the sand is the color of the sky on an unlucky day to marry. Painted on the door beneath the driver's casual left arm draped across the open window are words that can be assumed to reveal the truck's business. The driver keeps glancing into his rearview mirror then back at the opposite buildings, their obstinate facades unchanging. "Maspeth" is one of the words painted on the side of the truck, the letters overly bright like a deceptive explanation. Rugged is the profile of the driver who stares into the street through his window that is open like the heart of a woman who wants to be kissed. Behind me at the gym where I stand staring at a truck with small tanks filled with unknown liquids I can hear weights making metal sounds as I inhale the scent of perspired dreams. The driver yawns and runs his fingers through his dirty blond crew cut and the sleeve of his t-shirt slides along his tanned arm. The driver's profile does not resemble that of the bouncer guy who crosses paths with an actress on her way to the water fountain to my right. The ink on the driver's bicep spells "semper fi" in block letters, I can just make it out. Tick tock, I turn and touch my palms to the floor. Feeling the stretch in the muscles at the backs of my legs, I wonder about the unknown liquids and sand in a truck sitting outside the building where I am feeling the stretch in the muscles at the backs of my legs and wondering about the unknown liquids and sand in a truck sitting outside the building where I am feeling the stretch in the muscles at the backs of my legs and wondering about the unknown liquids and sand in a truck sitting outside the building where I am . . .

GROWING OLD

Once you were March,
Your life a rain-washed stoop,
A bruise that bloomed on a dancer's thigh

A mute passenger aboard a bus
Read tarot truths of discarded pride
As faith spewed from a tail pipe
And forgotten moments gathered in a silent storm

Today your future contains a tangerine lake
Drawn with fury by your former self
Your formal self
The you who longs and learns with rigor

They taught you happiness is relative
But you believe happiness is
A relative
The one who dictates your dreams from the after life

Now you are Autumn
Puberty taunts from a windswept shore
As Night opens on a progression of stars

PART TWO

TRAVELING

When I wake, I cannot remember the details of my dream
but an impression of a radiant journey remains. Now I am
aware of a man standing inside the curtained partition. His
gaze pins me. Immediate comprehension, no need to hear
his prepared speech. Only one word, "tumor," is
pronounced without obvious accent. I dress, distressed,
fingers fumble unable to entwine laces. A nurse, cigarette
hole puncturing the shoulder of her sweater, leads me to a
room devoid of joy: Patients high on propofol cannot leave
alone, she says, gesturing towards the others. She turns.
Disobeying the rules, I creep toward a red exit sign, lose
myself in a maze of disinfectant smells. The promised
alarm does not sound when I shove open the door. Concrete
path leads to subterranean entrance. Crumpled, I sit in the
only un-air-conditioned subway car.

my
body
has
betrayed
me

The train slides along a pair of tracks within a twisting
tunnel. Only a scientist peering through a microscope might
recognize how this underground journey strangely
resembles my genes—paired chromosomes riding a double
helix, traveling down the generations. Sunlight blinds me as
the train emerges from the tunnel to cross a bridge spanning
a polluted river. Again, I'm plunged into darkness. Minutes
later, I climb stairs, plod neglected avenues, arrive at an
infrequently visited address. Sobs when Sarah opens the
door. Her dog—rescued from abuse, rehabilitated with
love—licks my hand.

NAIVETE

dispel
the hysteria of
an answer to
a question unasked

the landslide of
conjunctions and clauses
remains amiss,
ignored, not listened to
except as possible cause

or curse

what is shadow if light
is both
a particle and a wave

residue of
dusty complaint

recognition of
imperfection as divine

acceptance of
this life as mine

DIRECTION

West is the river flowing like stop-
light-less traffic
and it murmurs a gentle riddle to you
standing alone on its profitless bank.

Tomorrow is a
slender boat
sailing beyond your
purposeless grasp.

Just then a casual breeze touches
your sunlit face
and all that you want to believe
holds sudden truth.

SLUM

In my wanderings today, I nearly stepped on a dead rat. My gaze was
inevitably drawn back to see how its insides had been squeezed out
through its anus as if, I suppose, it had been run over by a car. Though I
only briefly saw, I cannot now expel from my mind the colors of spilled
entrails, the sight of sharp teeth, the matted, greasy-looking fur . . .
And later, during evening mass while I sat in my pew, I thought about the
cruelty of nature, the destruction of hurricanes, electric slashes of
lightning in night-time skies, and how every animal and insect has its own
particular predator, its own particular prey. This is what God created, all of
it is His intention and because of this, I cannot believe there is not some
form of judgment after death. Such thoughts I have learned to call
religion, mine is a shared and practiced faith:

scent of incense
incantations
a madwoman scurrying among statues of the saints

CLEAN HANDS SAVE LIVES

reads the sign above the nurse's head
as she inserts another
insatiable needle.

The death of a dream is a sound like suction, the scent in the air is exhaust.

Mute injury marks
some of the faces waiting for treatment,
others appear merely stricken,
this decision
to be cured by toxic medications
must be lived with
all panic set aside.

In the neglected sky
an incomplete moon winks.

Are you strong enough for even this?

"I am, I
am!"
cries the bride of Occasional Morbidity,
soon wife of Euphoric Life.

AGGRESSIVE

Having abandoned one woman, the tumor slides beneath her door and crawls along the floor until it enters the catty-corner apartment where an even younger woman sleeps. Dreams flutter her eyelids, cause a muscle in her left leg to twitch once, twice, three times. Last year for five months her heart ballooned with love, a fully-inflated tire ready to begin a long journey. Then, poof! A puncture. In time, she recovered and began a new job in a distant district of the city. There her personality, an amoeba-like organism, divided into two leaving her with a new demeanor. Now as she travels underground on a rushing train, her breasts press into the bodies of others. Soon a test will be performed by a caffeinated technician who prefers Colombian blends, and, afterwards, a physician studying the film will detect a clump of malignant cells growing within her left breast. (The unopened window above his head reveals a sunset made brilliant by harmful emissions.) When it is dark, he leaves for home, a tidy apartment containing three TVs, two computers, and one wife. It has begun to drizzle. He finds the umbrella that he always carries at the bottom of his backpack. Again and again, he presses the plastic button but it refuses to unfurl. "Who made this?" he mutters as he walks through scattered rain drops. (Factory workers in a southern province of China.) While plummeting earthward, each separate raindrop becomes ever so slightly acidic, ever so slightly harmful to earth, yet nowhere near as lethal as the chemo soon to be endured by the younger woman in the catty-corner apartment who fell in love for five months last year.

MIGRATION ACROSS TIME

no lights
and slick
with rain
all roads require
faith
an affection for
complicity
the inner divinity
a feather
falling to earth
sin a wind
carrying the odor of decay

DIASPORA

The healing body is a sleeping
mind in a favored position on a sunlit
bed. Unwelcome wind sweeps the room, an
apparition of change that compels
with its touch.

My displaced tumor lives in exile
without passport, without creed:
homeless now it begs for
roof and root.

Outside the river waits
as a singular cloud, illuminated, pixelated, drifts
uncertainly across the passive
blue

Panic is a matter of
a few thronged moments of
despair
death-fear
disbelief.
No matter what
lives and lies
beyond this
moment
faith is wanted.

NUMB TERRAIN

My damp struggle
Ended
Apothecary's scorch remains
I will travel
This numb terrain
Help me excavate
Amygdala
Another self
Continues
Inviolable within
Folds of
Nebulae
Where prosperity
Reigns

SEED BOMB

In the mind
of someone loving
nervous angels sweep
the past from
accidental view while
repressed desires
dress in perfumed silk and
emerge as if on
cue and all
you dreamed when
you were wild
arises from
the sweet and
suspect river.

How do we bridge the
insurmountable?

How do we charm
distant eels?

In the heart of
someone sleeping
pastel zinnias
bloom and tremble
as they bathe in
waves of star shine
they are in awe of
heavenly fire
a universal core
you are unable
to deny
the fevered self
you once feared
might die.

AND AFTER THIS WHAT?

Somehow her encounter with death like dancing alone in the basement room of
some dank club made TRUTH more visceral   more visual   She didn't
dare avert her gaze from the smoking wreck of its message   She could not
abide the guy previously tolerable: his un-rightness for her had become neon in
force   the competitive *friend* a static banging noise ("The pipes fr cryin'
outloud!")   Whether her illness and attendant suffering had been a form
of penance or Job-like test, she had learned at least one thing: that she still
believed   Vague shame surrounded this weakness as others would
perceive it   sniggering behind her back   a superior sugary glaze coating their
eyes   and yet sometimes she felt proud of her   faith   in the
surrounding indiscriminate teeming persistence   (life)   Even more she
understood that she loved the earth   she breathed in scents of river and trees,
toking on the divine perfume   Above her mind a small machine
moved beneath gray clouds pregnant with rain   Is my end near or far? she
wondered   Purposeless flight, coveted night, fevers and storm
Placidity deceives, she told herself (a prim affixed to her grin): We are what
flows and
              falls

RECOVERED

In your desire to be open have you sacrificed instinct?
Constant truck with those who fail to inspire has left you cold.
Spring contains no heart, no pity —
It is a city anonymous in its needs.

A rainfall was found at the foot of a government high-rise.
Yesterday a witness arrived to confirm what others thought of you.
The bomb squad disappeared through revolving doors.

Winter leaves and leaves a feeling of derelict relief.
Meanwhile the surgeon Spring reaches inside of you.
As unclean hands stir dormant desires,
Your desperation is crushed beneath the blind man's boot.

COMPENSATIONS

You did not expect
Mercy to be grotesque and austere yet now that it is done
You understand it needed to be so

You are not alone in wondering
The meaning of a singing bird in the leafless tree
The persistent orbit of an arid moon

TOLD TO A STRANGER FAR FROM WHERE I LIVE

my birth certificate is filed inside a room where
sunlight is obscured by soot

at the edge of the town where
my birth certificate is filed
prison guards sleep

a tumor grows inside the lungs of
the clerk who notarized my birth certificate

in the town where my birth certificate is filed
citizens sit staring in
houses humming with machines built to feed, to
relax, to warm, to clean while
plastic bags wash up on its shore

signed by a doctor, a smudge mars
my birth certificate, a clumsy fold
creases its parchment

my birth certificate remains inside
a cabinet locked shut like
the minds of town daughters who learn early
to lie to their fathers and to confess to a priest

identical steel cabinets
hold death records and property deeds

on the street in the town where
my birth certificate sits within
color-coded file, children race home to
some mess of intimate
strangers known as family

the next-door town to the town where my birth certificate sleeps has been
abandoned by industry

in a synagogue across the street from
the building housing my birth certificate
a rabbi prays for
his addicted brother
clerks pass to and fro,
soiled thoughts echoing
within the airless room of my birth certificate

those who remain in the vicinity of my birth certificate
medicate themselves with
sweet-tasting pills prescribed by
grown boys once bullied by
mean boys whose fathers drank
all the pennies earned from piecework

tired ghosts rattle
the panes of snoring homes
as living hearts beat in unison . . .
and alone

TOLD TO A STRANGER NEAR TO WHERE THEY LIVE

those who remain medicate themselves with sweet-tasting pills
those who remain medicate themselves with sweet-tasting pills
those who remain medicate themselves with sweet-tasting pills
those who medicate themselves remain
those who medicate themselves remain sweet
medicate remain sweet
medicate remain
medicate remain sweet
those who medicate remain
medicate who
who who who
who remain who remain who remain
sweet-tasting pills
those sweet-tasting pills
those sweet-tasting pills remain
sweet-tasting pills medicate
sweet-tasting pills medicate those who remain sweet
sweet-tasting pills medicate those who remain
those who remain medicate themselves with sweet tasting pills and sleep
without dreaming then wake within the static of their lives
the static of their lives
static of
static of their
static
static
static
static
static

life

TOLD TO A STRANGER FAR FROM WHERE WE LIVE

Clouds pass briefly
overhead; we pause in
our assignments to
stare. These days
we live at
the southernmost edge of
the district beyond
houses, beyond
weary children, beyond
windows obscured by
soot. The eye returns
again and again to
beauty though
ugliness also has its
snares. To escape the
airborne toxic event, we
drove unsleek cars, habitually
changing lanes, infrequently
stopping to
compare.
Weakness, essential
to our nature, is our
strongest trait. This
work will soon become
another instrument of
futility, another
signpost of
future automation. The sounds
we make when laughing
are often brutal. We
have learned
who not to

touch and when to
pray. The taste
on our tongues
is remorse.

TOLD TO A STRANGER FAR FROM WHERE YOU LIVE

The birds return each spring
while citizens sit staring
in houses humming with machines.

Those without wings possess little more
than appetite, instinct and a particular
style of lust.

Infrequently your expert caution slips.
Each repressed impulse reveals
another symptom of decay.

Shrill winds rattle window panes
plastic bags wash up on the shore.
Beyond necessity, what will you do?

Your penultimate self
is obscured by distance. It
is a medicated spirit

fearing what might transpire
after
life.

TOLD TO A STRANGER NEAR TO WHERE I LIVE

While the children race home to
some mess of
intimate strangers known as
family
astronauts float in an international
space station
and particles
accelerate beneath
Switzerland.

I offer you newlywed vertigo, a quartet of moons, one spring expedition.

Let me rise like bread
to re-make my eternal bed.

Susan Scutti's poems appear in *The Outlaw Bible of American Poetry, Nuyorican Poets Cafe Anthology, Tin House Online, New York Quarterly, 2 Bridges Review, Oxford Quarterly, The Christian Science Monitor, Loose Change,* and a number of other journals and anthologies. Paper Kite Press published a full-length collection of her poems, *The Commute*; and Three Rooms Press published a chapbook, *We are Related*. Scutti is a graduate of Yale (BA) and City University of New York (MA). She lives in New York City.

www.ingramcontent.com/pod-product-compliance
Lightning Source LLC
Chambersburg PA
CBHW050659110426
42739CB00035B/3458